Level 4 – Blue

Helpful Hints for Reading at Home

The graphemes (written letters) and phonemes (units of sound) used throughout this series are aligned with Letters and Sounds. This offers a consistent approach to learning whether reading at home or in the classroom.

HERE IS A LIST OF PHONEMES FOR THIS PHASE OF LEARNING. AN EXAMPLE OF THE PRONUNCIATION CAN BE FOUND IN BRACKETS.

Phase 3			
j (jug)	v (van)	w (wet)	x (fox)
y (yellow)	z (zoo)	zz (buzz)	qu (quick)
ch (chip)	sh (shop)	th (thin/then)	ng (ring)
ai (rain)	ee (feet)	igh (night)	oa (boat)
oo (boot/look)	ar (farm)	or (for)	ur (hurt)
ow (cow)	oi (coin)	ear (dear)	air (fair)
ure (sure)	er (corner)		

HERE ARE SOME WORDS WHICH YOUR CHILD MAY FIND TRICKY.

Phase 3 Tricky Words			
he	you	she	they
we	all	me	are
be	my	was	her

TOP TIPS FOR HELPING YOUR CHILD TO READ:

- Allow children time to break down unfamiliar words into units of sound and then encourage children to string these sounds together to create the word.

- Encourage your child to point out any focus phonics when they are used.

- Read through the book more than once to grow confidence.

- Ask simple questions about the text to assess understanding.

- Encourage children to use illustrations as prompts.

This book focuses on the phonemes /or/ and /ur/ and is a blue level 4 book band.

Can you sort all the words on this page into two groups?

Cord

Turn

Words with **or**

Sort

For

Surf

Horn

Words with **ur**

Or

Return

All sorts of boats are at this port. Can you see them all?

This boat is at the port. It has lots of horns for the dark and the fog.

Horns

Boats can be big. This boat is big and long.

This boat is not big. It can fit a kid in.

Boats can be for a lot of things. They can be for fun or for jobs.

This sail boat is fun. It has a cord and big sails.

This is a tug boat. It is not big.

Tug Boat

It can tug things. It can tug a big boat and get it to turn.

Get the cord! This boat can tug a man. He can surf.

This kid can surf too. Look at her go!

Get the cord! We need to turn back to the port.

It is dark and hard to see. The torch will get us back.

Torch

©2022 **BookLife Publishing Ltd.**
King's Lynn, Norfolk PE30 4LS

ISBN 978-1-80155-100-7

All rights reserved. Printed in Poland.
A catalogue record for this book is available from the British Library.

Boats
Written by Madeline Tyler
Designed by Gareth Liddington

An Introduction to BookLife Readers...

Our Readers have been specifically created in line with the London Institute of Education's approach to book banding and are phonetically decodable and ordered to support each phase of Letters and Sounds.

Each book has been created to provide the best possible reading and learning experience. Our aim is to share our love of books with children, providing both emerging readers and prolific page-turners with beautiful books that are guaranteed to provoke interest and learning, regardless of ability.

BOOK BAND GRADED using the Institute of Education's approach to levelling.

PHONETICALLY DECODABLE supporting each phase of Letters and Sounds.

EXERCISES AND QUESTIONS to offer reinforcement and to ascertain comprehension.

CLEAR DESIGN to inspire and provoke engagement, providing the reader with clear visual representations of each non-fiction topic.

AUTHOR INSIGHT:
MADELINE TYLER

Native to Norfolk, England, Madeline Tyler's intelligence and professionalism can be felt in the 50-plus books that she has written for BookLife Publishing. A graduate of Queen Mary University of London with a 1st Class degree in Comparative Literature, she also received a University Volunteering Award for helping children to read at a local school.

When she was a child, Madeline enjoyed playing the violin, and she now relaxes through yoga and reading books!

This book focuses on the phonemes /or/ and /ur/ and is a blue level 4 book band.

Image Credits Images are courtesy of Shutterstock.com. With thanks to Getty Images, Thinkstock Photo and iStockphoto. Cover – 4&5 – Olga Donchuk, Melanie Lonbeck. 6&7 – 365 Focus Photography, Olga Lyubkin. 8&9 – tridland, PhotoSky. 10&11 – South Bay Lee, Triff. 12&13 – Galina Barskaya. 14&15 – Natali Glado, Valeriy Lebedev.